Keeping Clean

Eleanor Allen

Photographs by Maggie Murray
Illustrations by Sheila Jackson

A & C Black · London

First published by A & C Black (Publishers) Limited
35 Bedford Row, London WC1R 4JH

© 1991, A & C Black (Publishers) Limited
Reprinted 1991, 1992

ISBN 0 7136 3352 2

A CIP catalogue record for this book
is available from the British Library.

Filmset by August Filmsetting, Haydock, St Helens
Printed in Italy by Amadeus

Acknowledgements

The author and publisher would like to thank the following
people for their valuable help during the preparation of this
book: Dr Simon Penn, curator of Avoncroft Museum of
Buildings; Mrs Margaret Mallen of Sudeley Castle; and Suella
Postles of Brewhouse Yard Museum, for making it possible for
us to photograph items from those collections. They would also
like to thank Mr Greaney and the staff of Moseley Road
Swimming Baths, Birmingham; and Miss Shee, and children
Max, Jonathan, Sabina and Sarah–Jane of St George's RC
Primary School, Worcester.

Photographs by Maggie Murray except for: p25 (top) Buckley's
Shop Museum, Battle, Sussex; p5, 10 (bottom), 17 (top), 20
(bottom), 22 (bottom) Mary Evans Picture Library; p1 The
Greater London Photographic Library; p12 (top) The Hulton–
Deutsch Collection; p24 (bottom) Ian Moir; p20 (top), Robert Opie.

Contents

How do you keep yourself clean?

Do you have to be forced into the bathroom sometimes? Does brushing your teeth, washing your hands and face, having a bath, or maybe washing your hair before school, seem too much of an effort? Do you actually need to think about what you are doing, or can you get yourself clean while still half-asleep?

▲ A modern bathroom would have seemed very luxurious to poorer people at the turn of the century. Most of them had to wash in the kitchen.

We find it easy to keep clean. But at the turn of the century, when your great grandma was young, people found it much harder. Bathrooms fitted with all the things most people take for granted, like hot running water, baths, washbasins and flushing lavatories, were luxuries which only a few very rich people could afford.

Special rooms set aside for bathing were quite a new idea. They only dated back to around 1880. People who had a bathroom were very proud of it. Many homes not only didn't have a bathroom or indoor lavatory of any sort – they didn't even have a water tap in the house.

Time-line

	pre-1880s	1880s	1890s	1900s	1910s	1920s
		Great great grandparents were born		Great grandparents were born		
Important events	**1870** Alexander Graham Bell invents telephone	**1888** Dunlop invents pneumatic tyre	**1890** Moving pictures start **1896** First modern Olympic Games	**1901** Queen Victoria dies. Edward VII becomes King **1903** Wright brothers fly first plane	**1910** George V becomes King **1914–18** World War I	**1926** Gener[e] Strike in Britain
Keeping clean dates	**1778** The first WCs to be manufactured in large numbers went on sale. Six thousand were made by Joseph Bramah, a London cabinet-maker ● Outbreaks of diseases, such as cholera and typhoid, led to the passing of several Public Health Acts in the second half of the 19th century. As a result towns and cities began to improve their sewerage systems **1852** First gents public lavatory opened	**1880** Perforated toilet roll invented ● Cast iron baths came into use ● Introduction of flushing lavatories with pedestal closet and high cistern ● Purpose-designed bathrooms introduced **1881** First-class railway carriages were fitted with WCs by the Midland Railway Company **1886** The Manchester, Sheffield and Lincolnshire Railway fitted their third-class railway carriages with WCs	**1890s** Experiments in use of bacteria to break down sewage (This method still in use) **1891** Toothpaste in a tube first introduced into Britain **1894** Lifebuoy soap introduced ● Railway companies began building public lavatories at railway stations	**1900s** Bathrooms become more practical with piped water and water heaters **1905** Chlorination of water slowly introduced on a routine basis to fight water-borne diseases	**1913** The first aeroplane fitted with a toilet flew in Russia **1919** The first airliner fitted with a WC flew on a regular route from London to Paris	**1920s** Some council hous[e] and flats started to h[o] bathrooms

6

This time-line shows some of the important events since your great grandparents were children, and some of the events and inventions which have changed the ways in which we keep ourselves clean.

randparents were born		Parents were born		You were born		
930	1940s	1950s	1960s	1970s	1980s	1990s
Edward bdicates. rge VI omes King irst vision dcasts World II starts	**1941** Penicillin successfully tested **1945** World War II ends **1947** First supersonic plane	**1952** Elizabeth II becomes Queen **EIIR** **1959** Yuri Gagarin first man in space	**1969** Neil Armstrong first man on the moon	**1973** Britain enters the Common Market	**1981** First successful space shuttle flight	
s Lavatory r ming e widely ibbs SR paste duced in in rass taps g way to e easily- ed mium d ones e 'low- ' WC (first duced in 890s) n to ce toilets overhead ing tanks	**1942** Soap rationing was introduced during World War II SOAP FLAKES	**1950s** Over one-third of all dwellings over the whole of the UK were still without bathrooms **1955** Roll-on deodorant introduced	**1962** Aerosol deodorant introduced to the UK • Coloured bathroom suites became popular • Fluoride toothpaste introduced	**1971** The introduction of decimal currency ended the penny charge at many public lavatories • Coloured lavatory rolls became popular to match coloured bathroom suites	**1980** Jacuzzi and whirlpool baths introduced • Aerosol deodorants began to fall from favour because of the damage to the ozone layer caused by the CFC propellants used in them • A return of interest in older designs of bathrooms	

Bathing in the kitchen

▲ These children tried pumping water from a well. They found it was very hard work.

At the turn of the century, very few families had water piped into their homes; people couldn't just turn on a tap to fill their bath. They had to collect every drop of water they needed from an outside tap, which was often shared with other families, and then carry the heavy metal buckets inside. Some people had to take their water from a well, a pump, or even from a rainwater butt which stored water from the roof.

Collecting all the buckets of water needed to fill a bath was back-breaking work, especially for a mother whose children were too small to help.

◄ The tide mark round this old tin bath suggests that people usually bathed with it less than half full. The buckets of water were so heavy, the children decided they would stop when the bath was less than half full.

Once the water had been carried inside, it had to be heated. This was done either by pouring it into the copper, a large metal container in which water for washing clothes was heated, or by filling large pans which were then heated on the kitchen fire or on the range.

Very few people had bathrooms, so your great grandma probably bathed in front of the kitchen fire in a tin bath. Even large tin baths were too short for an adult to lie in. Bathers had to sit up, usually with their knees drawn up in front of them. The empty bath was an awkward thing to store in a small house. It was usually hung outside on a hook by the door where it blew and rattled in the wind.

▼ This tin bath is hanging on the wall next to the rainwater butt outside an old toll house which has been reconstructed at Avoncroft Museum of Buildings. This is where the bath would have been kept at the turn of the century.

▲ People who had no tin bath used the wooden clothes washing tub and bathed their babies in the washing-up bowl. The copper, which provided the hot water for washing clothes, stands in the corner.

This girl tried out the tin bath, with the clothes horse as a screen, in the kitchen at Brewhouse Yard Museum, Nottingham. The room is equipped with furniture and kitchen items from the turn of the century, so this is how bath night would have looked a hundred years ago.

It was warm and cosy in front of the kitchen fire, with the clothes horse pulled round to keep off the draughts. However, the kitchen was often also the main, or only living room, where everybody sat. In houses with large families, it was difficult to be private.

Mrs Smith, who was a child at the turn of the century, explains how her family coped:

'Our bath night was Friday. Dad went up early on Fridays to give us girls some privacy. We pulled the clothes horse round, with the washing hanging on it, and used it for a screen. But it wasn't very private, was it? Not like being able to lock yourself in the bathroom...'

▲ This cartoon dates from 1896. The water tap, which was shared by all those people, was only turned on for a certain length of time each day. The heavy metal object the man is holding is the key for turning it on. The women are carrying jugs and kettles in which to carry the water home.

Getting a bath ready and emptying it away afterwards took so much time, that it couldn't be done on the spur of the moment. Once a bath had been prepared, the water was put to full use. Children were put in one after the other, starting with the cleanest. In most houses the children not only used the same water, they also used the same towel. Doing the laundry was hard work and few mothers were prepared to provide a dry towel for everybody. When the towel became too wet, they dried on their dirty underclothes.

A once-weekly bath was usual, with the whole evening set aside for it. But lots of people bathed far less frequently, especially those who were old or sick, or children in families where the mother didn't have time for all the extra work. Many never had a proper bath. In summer they had an occasional wash-down, using a bowl. In winter they didn't bother.

▼ These boys found that emptying the bath was very hard work. The water swished from side to side and they had to be very careful not to spill any on to the floor.

Washing in the bedroom

Some people preferred to bathe in the privacy of the bedroom, but this caused an enormous amount of extra inconvenience and hard work. All the water, both hot and cold, had to be carried upstairs. Afterwards, unless there was a gutter within easy reach, it had to be emptied back into containers and carried downstairs to be tipped away.

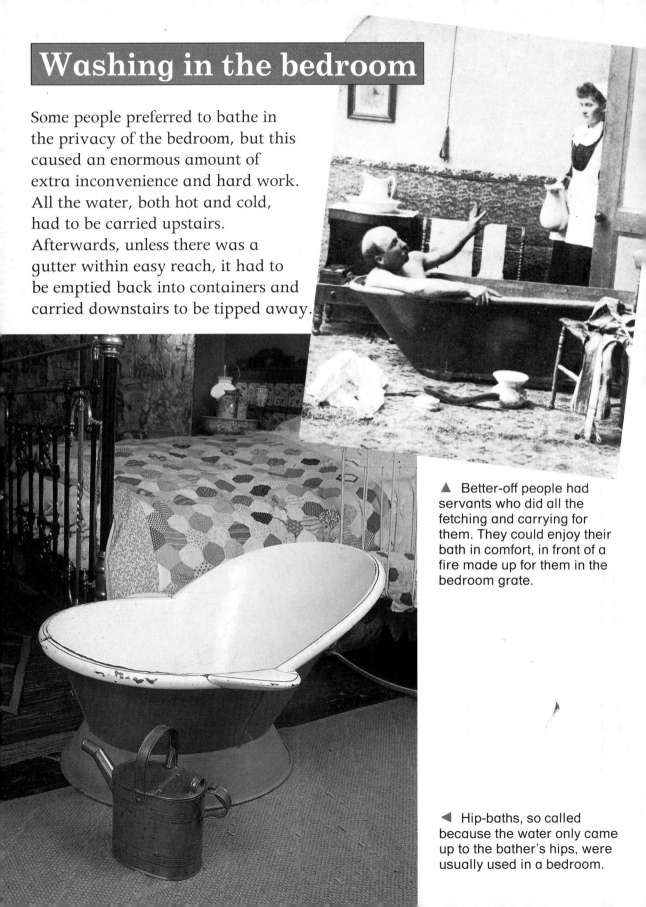

▲ Better-off people had servants who did all the fetching and carrying for them. They could enjoy their bath in comfort, in front of a fire made up for them in the bedroom grate.

◄ Hip-baths, so called because the water only came up to the bather's hips, were usually used in a bedroom.

Other people did not go to the trouble of having a bath. They had a good all-over wash, or cleaned just their hands and faces, using only one jug of warm water. Great grandma used a piece of furniture which was specially made for washing. It was called a washstand and looked rather like a dressing table. A large bowl and matching jug stood on the marble top. Underneath was a slop bucket with a lid, into which the dirty water was poured. Towels were hung on a wooden towel rail next to the washstand.

▶ A porcelain slop bucket. The bowl-shaped lid and the holes in the middle meant that dirty water could be tipped into the bucket without the lid being removed.

▲ Many washstands had splashbacks decorated with attractive tiles like this one at the Brewhouse Yard Museum, Nottingham. The copper can is for carrying hot water up and down stairs.

13

Public bath houses

During Victorian times, scientists realised that dirt was a breeding ground for the germs which caused infections and disease. Doctors began to wash carefully before examining patients or operating on them. Children were taught about hygiene in school. People in authority, following the saying that 'cleanliness is next to godliness', were very keen to encourage everybody to wash and bathe regularly.

To help those people living in poor, overcrowded households where it was difficult to keep clean, some town and city councils decided to build public bath houses.

▼ The children went to visit a Victorian bath house at Moseley in Birmingham.

▲ Each cubicle contained a bath, a folding seat for putting clothes on, and a small wooden duckboard so that bathers wouldn't slip on the marble floor.

▲ They thought the bath house must have seemed like a palace to people who were used to bathing in front of the kitchen fire.

They made the bath houses as attractive and luxurious as possible with colourful tiles, marble and polished wood. Anyone wanting to wash could hire a cubicle containing a large, deep bath with hot and cold running water. It cost about 2*d* or 4*d* for half an hour, depending on whether they went First or Second class. Although that doesn't sound very much, poor people could not afford to go very often.

The idea of public bath houses wasn't new – it dated back to Roman times. Like the Romans, the Victorians built swimming baths alongside their bath houses. The swimming baths soon became more popular than the public baths. The local authorities who built them had to be content with the thought that they at least encouraged many 'to bathe occasionally, who would otherwise never wash'.

Many people used public bath houses because they were too old or sick to prepare a bath at home. In case they were taken ill in the bath, a bell pull was provided, and there was a stout rope to help people haul themselves out of the deep tub.

Most public bath houses have been demolished, but a few, like the one at Moseley, Birmingham, are still in use. There is little demand for bath houses these days, but at the turn of the century, on a Saturday morning people had to queue to use them.   15

A proper bathroom

At the turn of the century some well-off people, who had large houses with piped water, began to convert their spare bedrooms into bathrooms. These were often decorated in the same way as bedrooms, with carpet on the floor, pictures on the walls and heavy curtains at the windows. The bathroom fittings, which were big and solid, were often encased in wood. The bath and washbasin usually had heavy taps.

After the turn of the century, as more people had piped water in their homes, some new, larger houses were built with specially designed bathrooms. These bathrooms were still very comfortable, but they were brighter and easier to keep clean.

▼ The children investigated a turn of the century bathroom at Sudeley Castle. The bath and basin had a matching lavatory, which was unusual then. The room was panelled in a rich, dark wood called mahogany. Can you spot any other differences between this room and a modern bathroom?

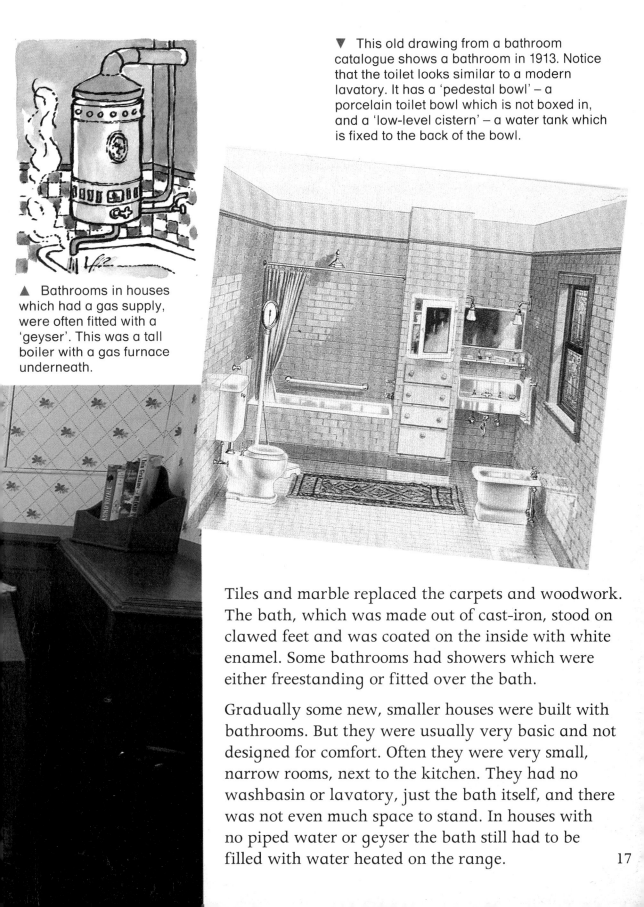

▼ This old drawing from a bathroom catalogue shows a bathroom in 1913. Notice that the toilet looks similar to a modern lavatory. It has a 'pedestal bowl' – a porcelain toilet bowl which is not boxed in, and a 'low-level cistern' – a water tank which is fixed to the back of the bowl.

▲ Bathrooms in houses which had a gas supply, were often fitted with a 'geyser'. This was a tall boiler with a gas furnace underneath.

Tiles and marble replaced the carpets and woodwork. The bath, which was made out of cast-iron, stood on clawed feet and was coated on the inside with white enamel. Some bathrooms had showers which were either freestanding or fitted over the bath.

Gradually some new, smaller houses were built with bathrooms. But they were usually very basic and not designed for comfort. Often they were very small, narrow rooms, next to the kitchen. They had no washbasin or lavatory, just the bath itself, and there was not even much space to stand. In houses with no piped water or geyser the bath still had to be filled with water heated on the range.

17

Washing your hair

Great grandma would have been amazed to see the vast array of shampoos, hair conditioners and styling lotions on sale in the shops today. Most people in her day washed their hair with ordinary soap.

Mrs Goodwin, who was born in 1900, remembers:

'We never knew what shampoo was then in our family, I can't remember anybody I knew using it.'

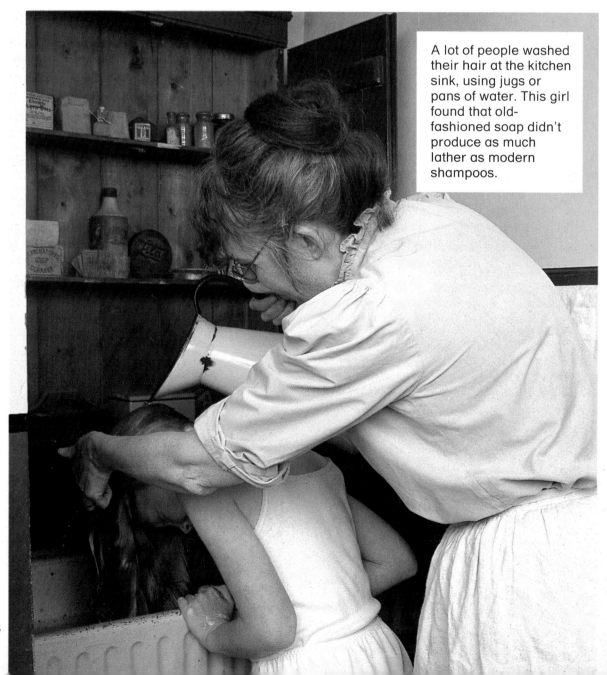

A lot of people washed their hair at the kitchen sink, using jugs or pans of water. This girl found that old-fashioned soap didn't produce as much lather as modern shampoos.

▲ For special occasions, ringlets were popular for young girls. They were made by twisting strands of hair round long strips of rag, forming what were called 'sore fingers'. To get perfect ringlets, you had to sleep with the sore fingers in place.

▲ The girl found her hair felt stiff and uncomfortable after being washed in soap. She spent quarter of an hour trying to dry it with a towel, and then gave up and used a hair dryer!

▼ Some elaborate hair-dos required the use of curling tongs. These were heated over a spirit lamp. A piece of tissue paper was folded over each strand of dry hair before it was curled round the tongs.

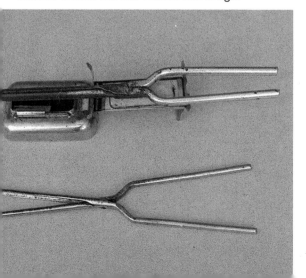

Many people washed their hair in the bath, placing extra pans of clean water for rinsing within easy reach on the floor. Rainwater was favoured for rinsing hair because it was soft and left the hair shiny. Poorer people didn't bother with special conditioners, but sometimes added a teaspoon or so of vinegar or lemon juice to the rinsing water to neutralise the alkali of the soap. At the turn of the century, long hair was the fashion for women and girls. There were no hair dryers, so drying long hair took ages. Mrs Goodwin told the children:

'If you were washing your hair, it took all evening. You couldn't wash your hair then go out, like today. You had to sit in front of the kitchen fire brushing it dry, or just let it dry naturally. My husband had seven sisters, all with long hair. Because he was the youngest brother, he had to help them brush it dry. He always remembered that – all the girls drying their lovely long hair in front of the fire.'

Bathroom bits and pieces

Many of the things you use to help you smell clean and fresh hadn't been invented in great grandma's day. People could buy toilet soap, some with the same brand names we know today, such as Lifebuoy and Pears. But these soaps were a luxury. Many households could only afford to bathe with the same coarse soap they used for washing clothes.

On special occasions people might sprinkle herbs into the bath, or add some powdered borax to soften the water. But generally people didn't bother to add anything to the bath water.

There were no deodorants or anti-perspirants to put on after a bath, though many people used talcum powder. Some people concocted their own, but most didn't see the need. Body odour was just a fact of life. Some dresses had pads sewn in under the armpits to collect sweat, but as Mrs Phillips, who was a young girl at the turn of the century, points out:

'It was generally best dresses that had them sewn in, so it was just to protect the fabric from staining, rather than for any hygienic purpose.'

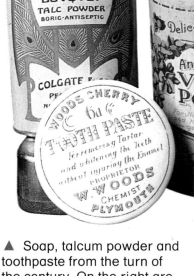

▲ Soap, talcum powder and toothpaste from the turn of the century. On the right are bottles containing an anti-dandruff preparation and hair restorer.

◀ There were big advertising campaigns for Lifebuoy and Pears around the turn of the century.

People then didn't pay so much attention to brushing their teeth as we do. Lots of people who kept themselves quite clean in other ways, never brushed their teeth at all, as Mrs Goodwin remembers:

'Do you know, I can't remember brushing my teeth when I was young. I don't think we ever did. We only had the kitchen sink, you see. And it would have meant a toothbrush for each of us, wouldn't it, and I'm sure we didn't have that. I remember that rubbing them with salt on a bit of rag was supposed to clean them – or soot. Yes – soot! I think I tried that once, but I don't know if it did any good. I had false teeth in my twenties. A lot of us did in those days – there's no wonder, is there?'

Toothbrushes and toothpaste could be bought at the chemist by people who could afford such luxuries. Toothpaste in a tube hadn't been invented. It was sold as a powder or as a solid block in a tin or a jar. You rubbed a wet toothbrush over it until enough of it had stuck to the bristles.

▼ A set of ivory bathroom items from the turn of the century. On the left is a talcum powder shaker. Toothbrush bristles were often made of pig's hair.

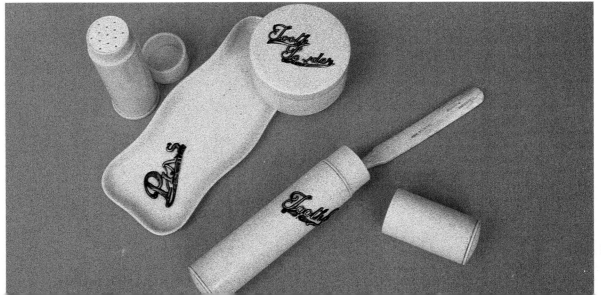

Outdoor lavatories

A hundred years ago most people had to use an outside lavatory. In country areas this was usually housed in a shed at the bottom of the garden. In cities the lavatories were put in the back yards which separated the rows of houses. These outside lavatories were called 'privies', but they weren't very private. In towns everybody could see their neighbours crossing the yard to use them.

Some families had to share a lavatory with several others. In the 1890s, a London doctor reported a case of only one lavatory for 25 houses. Everybody, had to queue up before going to work or school.

▲ A country privy. On dark winter evenings people had to carry a candle or a paraffin lantern to light their way to the toilet.

▲ A town privy. In very crowded areas the privies were built in rows, sometimes containing a dozen or more lavatories.

Around the turn of the century most privies were fitted with earth closets. Each had a wide wooden seat with a round hole in the middle. Some privies had two or three holes in a row, of varying sizes, for different members of the family. A small, child's hole was sometimes constructed on a lower level.

Underneath the wooden seat was a large pit dug in the earth into which the sewage fell. Dry earth, or ashes from the hearth, were stored, either in a box next to the closet, or in a container above the seat. When people finished using the lavatory, they scooped earth or ashes from the box and sprinkled some down the hole to kill the smell.

▶ If an earth closet was built close to a well, it could be a grave health hazard. Sewage from an unlined pit could seep into the water supply, causing killer diseases like typhoid.

▲ Pits were emptied by workers using tools which looked like giant spoons. The shaft of the spoon was wooden and the bowl was metal.

This splended 3-seater lavatory has been reconstructed at Avoncroft Museum of Buildings. It is over 200 years old, but the same type of lavatory was in general use at the turn of the century. The children are looking down the centre hole into the deep, brick-lined pit. There are many tales of small children sitting on a large, adult's hole and falling through!

▲ A trap door was constructed at the front so that the bucket could be easily removed.

▼ The workers who emptied the lavatories, and their cart with bins full of sewage.

Gradually bucket closets replaced these earth closets. The big pit was filled in and concreted over. The new lavatories, which had a large bucket positioned under the wooden seat, were healthier because the buckets could be emptied daily.

In towns the buckets were put out at night to be emptied. A horse-drawn cart rattled up the road late at night or early in the morning, carrying a collection of steel drums into which the sewage was poured. In some country areas there was no collection. People had to get rid of the sewage wherever they could. Emptying the buckets was usually Father's job. When he got home from work he had to dig a hole in the garden and tip the contents of the bucket into it.

► This inside lavatory at Buckley's Shop Museum, Sussex, originally had an ash box. At the turn of the century, it was converted to a water flush with a high cistern. Notice the small child's seat, and the paraffin lamp on the shelf. There are two sorts of lavatory paper – newspaper squares and a more modern perforated roll.

Outdoor lavatories were cold and draughty in winter, and in the height of summer they were plagued by flies. The flies weren't just a nuisance, they spread germs and diseases. Summer attacks of diarrhoea were common amongst all age groups, but for babies they could be fatal. During an epidemic in the summer of 1911, nearly 30,000 babies died.

A more hygienic type of lavatory, called the water closet or WC, had been invented in 1589, by Sir John Harrington. This had a porcelain pan with an S-shaped water-filled trap in the base to prevent smells coming into the room. The sewage was washed away with a flush of water.

These lavatories did not come into general use for a long time. This was because in order to work properly, they needed water piped into the houses, and sewage pipes going out to large sewers to carry away the waste. The difficulties and expense involved in laying extra water pipes and constructing miles of sewers, meant that towns were slow to convert to water closets. Many country areas and city slums continued to use pits and pails, until well after World War II.

Going inside

A hundred years ago families with indoor water closets were few and far between, and usually very rich. WCs often had a cistern mounted high on the wall, attached by a pipe to a china closet which was either boxed in with wood or sometimes ornately decorated. The seat and lid were made of wood, either pine, which could be scrubbed clean, or polished mahogany. The flush was worked by a long chain which was attached to the cistern.

You might have thought that everybody who could afford to install an indoor WC would have been keen to do so. But that wasn't the case. Some people believed it was unhygienic to have one indoors. Mrs Goodwin remembers that in about 1910 the owner of her local village shop swore he would never have a WC put in.

'He said they were dirty, smelly places and fancy putting one in your house – they belonged outside!'

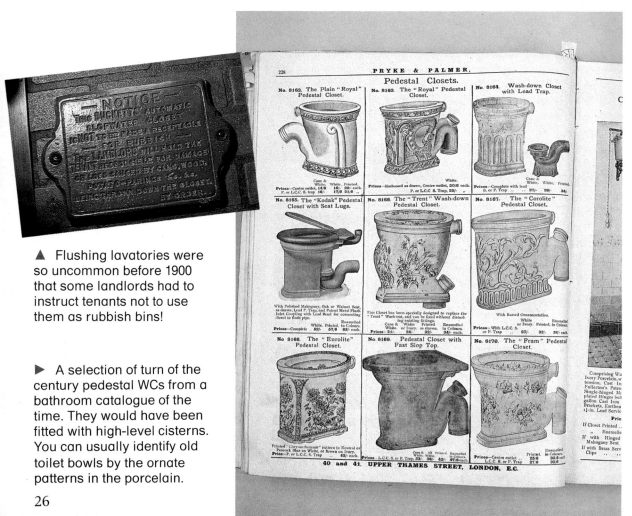

▲ Flushing lavatories were so uncommon before 1900 that some landlords had to instruct tenants not to use them as rubbish bins!

▶ A selection of turn of the century pedestal WCs from a bathroom catalogue of the time. They would have been fitted with high-level cisterns. You can usually identify old toilet bowls by the ornate patterns in the porcelain.

Turn of the century chamber pot with lid ▽

◁ enamel chamber pot

△ Willow pattern pot

Chamber pots were usually made of porcelain and were prettily decorated. You could buy plain enamel ones, which some people preferred for the reason Mrs Goodwin points out: 'When we were children, my mother made us use enamel potties. I think it was because they were safer. A woman who was looking after us had once sat on a porcelain one and it broke and cut her bottom.'

Queen Victoria's Jubilee ▽

1837 1887

Marble ware chamber pot ▽

People with no indoor lavatory, who needed to go in the night, used a chamber pot. All homes had them, tucked away under the bed, or stored in a simple wooden cupboard. They were used only in an emergency because it wasn't very healthy or pleasant to sleep in the same room as a used potty. Boys and men often solved the problem by peeing out of the window.

Nobody enjoyed the job of emptying the potties in the morning. Mrs Phillips remembers:

'I can remember having to help my mother by emptying the potties from under the beds every morning. I had to tip them all out into a bucket, then carry the bucket downstairs and down the garden to the privy. Then I had to put some clean water and disinfectant in the bucket and go back and rinse them out, ready for the next night.'

Chamberpot 1930

Lavatory paper

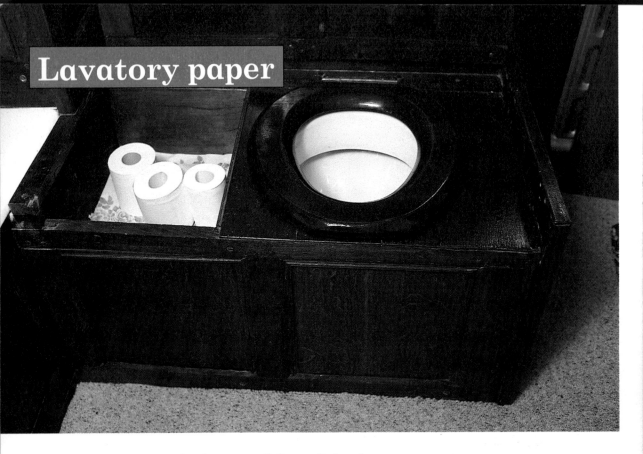

Some bathrooms in the houses of the rich had specially bought lavatory paper. It came in stiff paper squares and was usually kept in small boxes made of ornately decorated pottery or polished wood.

The first perforated lavatory roll was invented in the 1880s, but they took a long time to become popular. Soft lavatory paper was not widely used in British homes until the 1950s.

Most people, even in quite well-off households, used newspaper. It was often the children's job to cut old copies of the family newspapers into useable sized squares, string them together and fasten them on a hook behind the lavatory door. Mrs Phillips remembers:

'You'd be sitting on the loo and your eye would be caught by a headline and you'd set off reading ... You could be hours in there. Sometimes you only got to read half an article because the rest had been torn off and used ...'

▲ The lavatory in the bathroom at Sudeley Castle has a space for lavatory paper under the lid. With the lid down it looks like a seat or chest. The rolls shown here are modern.

Public lavatories

Public WCs, which people could pay to use, were still quite a new thing at the turn of the century. They had become necessary because easier methods of transport meant that people were spending longer hours away from home, on day trips and shopping expeditions.

Some of the largest and most elaborate public lavatories were built by railway companies for their passengers. Most trains at that time didn't have corridors, so travellers had to stay in their compartments until the end of the journey, then make a dash for the station lavatory.

▲ Street lavatories were also built in major towns and cities. Like this one in Birmingham, they were often underground where they would not be 'eye-sores'.

▶ A Victorian public urinal in Birmingham. Notice the decorated cast-iron panels which shielded the users from the gaze of passers-by, the lack of a roof and the pipe which connects the urinal directly to the main sewers.

How to find out more

Start here	To find out about . . .	Who will have . . .
Old people	Keeping clean at the turn of the century	Old photos, scrap books, old washing equipment
Junk shops	What people bought	Old catalogues, old magazines and old cards showing people washing; washing equipment, chamber pots
Museums	Old things to look at and possibly to handle	Reconstructed bathrooms, displays of washing equipment
Libraries	● Loan collections ● Reference collections ● Information to help your research ● Local history section	● Books to borrow ● Books, magazines, newspapers ● Useful addresses, guide books, additional reference material ● Newspapers and guides to look at. Photographs of local people, public toilets etc
Country houses and stately homes	Rich people's bathrooms and toilets	Original bathrooms, toilets, wash-stands, chamber pots and toiletries
Manufacturers of toiletries and bathroom equipment	The history of their products	Old catalogues, an official company history or ideas about where to go for more information

Who can tell you more?

They can. Use a tape recorder for recording their memories. Handle anything they show you with great care and if they lend you something, label it with their name and keep it somewhere safe

The owner. Specialist shopkeepers are usually very enthusiastic and knowledgeable about their stock. They may know of local people with collections of things connected with keeping clean. They may be able to give you further contacts and addresses

The curator or the museum's education officer. Many museums have bookshops and a notice board where it would be worth looking for further information

- The librarian.
- The reference librarian.
- Ask the archivist for the name and address of the local history society

The guide or guide book

The information officer or public relations officer. Write to them for information

Places to visit

Many local museums, particularly folk museums, and country houses which are open to the public have small displays or single items connected with keeping clean or hygiene.

The following places have displays, reconstructions or exhibitions connected with this subject:

Abbey House Museum, Abbey Road, Kirkstall, Leeds, West Yorkshire LS5 3EH. Tel: 0532–755821
Avoncroft Museum of Buildings, Bromsgrove, Hereford and Worcester B60 4JR. Tel: 0527–31363
Brewhouse Yard Museum, Castle Boulevard, Nottingham NG7 1FB. Tel: 0602–483504
Blists Hill Open Air Museum, Ironbridge, Telford, Shropshire TF8 7AW. Tel: 095245–3522
Gladstone Pottery Museum, Uttoxeter Road, Longton, Stoke-on-Trent, Staffordshire ST3 1PQ. Tel: 0782–319232.
Newby Hall, Ripon, North Yorkshire HG4 5AE. Tel: 09012–2583. This has the finest exhibition of chamber pots in the country.
Sudeley Castle, Winchcombe, Gloucestershire. Tel: 0242–602308

Index